Contents

1 A man called Muhammad	4	
2 Muhammad's Message	6	
3 Islam Spreads	8	
4 Holy Book – the Qur'an	10	
5 What Muslims Believe	12	
6 Prayer	14	
7 At the Mosque	16	
8 Imams	18	
9 Zakat (alms)	20	
10 Sawm (fasting)	22	
11 Hajj (pilgrimage)	24	
12 Birth and Death	26	
13 Getting Married	28	
14 Family Life	30	
15 Muslim Women	32	
16 Muslim Festivals	34	
17 Daily Life	36	
18 Food and Drink	38	
19 Muslim Groups	40	
20 Islam's Gifts to the World	42	
21 Islam Today	44	
Connections	46	
Glossary	47	
Index	48	

Author's note

Whenever Muslims speak or write Muhammad's name, they usually add, 'Peace be upon him'. (Sometimes written as 'pbuh'.) It is a sign of respect. This book does not do so, but this is not intended to be disrespectful. A Muslim who reads aloud from this book may wish to add these words wherever the Prophet's name occurs.

A man called Muhammad

About the year 570 CE a baby boy was born in Makkah (Mecca), in what is now Saudi Arabia. The boy was Muhammad.

His father had died weeks earlier. It was the custom in his tribe for new-born babies to be fed by a **foster-mother**. So at first Muhammad was looked after by a **Bedouin** woman.

When he was six, his mother died and he went to live with his grandfather. Just two years later, his grandfather also died and Muhammad was looked after by his uncle, a merchant.

As a boy, Muhammad looked after sheep in the desert. When he grew up, he was proud of this work. '**Allah**,' he told people, 'sent no **prophet** who was not a shepherd.'

Muhammad went on to become a camel driver and, later, a trader. He was honest and a hard worker and was spotted by a rich widow called Khadijah. She was a trader and asked him to look after her business affairs.

He was a good businessman. On his first trip to Syria, he earned Khadijah nearly twice the money that she expected. Soon afterwards, she asked Muhammad to marry her.

Muhammad's uncle advised the young man to accept. So, aged 25, Muhammad married Khadijah, who was older than him. It was a happy marriage. They had seven children, three boys and four girls.

Muslims believe that a Christian monk had foretold that Muhammad would become a prophet. Now came an event which showed people how wise this young man was.

Makkah was already a religious city. **Pilgrims** flocked to see the black stone which was kept in the **Ka'bah**. The Arabs believed it was sent from the sky. One year, heavy rain damaged the walls of the Ka'bah; repairs were needed. Four tribes would share the work.

This old picture shows a Muslim merchant setting off on a journey.

The Muslim Experience

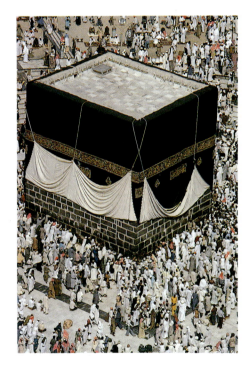

J F Aylett

Hodder & Stoughton

A MEMBER OF THE HODDER HEADLINE GROUP

Acknowledgements

The Publishers would like to thank the following for permission to reproduce material in this volume:

BBC Radio for the extract from *Quest*; BBC Television for the extract from *Third Eye* (1982); Christian Education Movement for the extract from *RE Today*; Channel Four Television Company Ltd for the extract from *Muslims in Britain* – a Priory Production for Channel 4 Television Company Ltd; The Muslim Educational Trust for the extracts from *The 4th Revised Edition of Islam Beliefs and Teachings* (1989); Time Life Books Inc for the extract from *Great Ages of Man: Early Islam* by Desmond Stewart and the Editors of Time-Life Books, © 1967 Time-Life Books Inc; TVS Production Ltd for the extract from their *Human Factor* programme (1988); Unwin Hyman Ltd for the extract from *Rugs to Riches* by Caroline Bosley (1981).

Every effort has been made to trace and acknowledge ownership of copyright. The publishers will be glad to make suitable arrangements with any copyright holders whom it has not been possible to contact.

The Publishers would like to thank the following for their permission to reproduce the following copyright photographs in this book:

Mohamed Ansar – pp16l.; 18r.; 21; 27; 37, Associated Press – pp38r.; 44l, La Bibliotheque Nationale – p4, Sonia Halliday Photographs – pp9; 12r.; 33, NAAS – pp30r.; 36r.; 40r.; cover, New York Public Library – p6, Christine Osborne/Middle East Pictures – pp16r.; 18l.; 30l.; 31; 32r.; 34r.; 36l, Ann and Bury Peerless – pp25; 32l., Peter Sanders – pp12l.; 23; 26; 29; 38l., Topham Picture Source – pp28; 41, Topham Picture Source/Christine Osborne – p40l., Topkapi Palace Museum – p10, Tropix Photographic Library – p19.

To Nicolas, in friendship and with gratitude.

British Library Cataloguing in Publication Data
Aylett, J.F.
  Seeking Religion: the Muslim experience
  — (Seeking Religion)
  I. Title   II. Series
  297

ISBN 0 340 49375-5

First published 1991
Impression number   13 12 11 10 9 8 7 6
Year   1999 1998 1997 1996

Typeset by Taurus Graphics, Abingdon, Oxon.
Printed in Hong Kong for Hodder & Stoughton Educational, a division of Hodder Headline Plc, 338 Euston Road, London NW1 3BH by Colorcraft Ltd., Hong Kong.

All went well until the time came to put the black stone in place. Then the arguments began. Which tribe should have the honour of doing it? The quarrels were so bitter that it even looked as though a **civil war** might break out.

In the end, an old man had an idea. They would let the gods help. The first person to walk through the temple gates next day would be asked to sort it out. The first person turned out to be Muhammad.

People already called him 'the honest one'. So he seemed a good person to solve the dispute. His solution was very clever. He took a cloak and spread it on the ground. The black stone was placed on top and leaders from each tribe took hold of the corners of the cloak. Holding tight, they lifted the stone into place. Then, Muhammad slid it into position.

From then onwards, Muhammad spent more time **meditating**. He was upset by the way the people of Makkah lived their lives. He wanted to be alone to think. Each year, during the month of Ramadan, he went alone to a cave on Mount Hira, outside the city. He did this until he was forty years old. That year was his fifth at the cave – and he had a surprise visitor.

▶ **Handsome; medium height; thick black hair and beard; wide forehead; heavy eyebrows; large dark eyes below long lashes; wide chest and shoulders.**

Muslims do not draw pictures of Muhammad. They believe it is wrong. But their holy books give this description of him.

These modern Muslims are making a pilgrimage to Mount Hira. They believe this was Muhammad's cave.

1 Copy out and complete this paragraph:
   Muhammad's mother died when he was _____ and he was later looked after by an _____ . He worked as a _____ and later with camels. Aged 25, he married _____ and they had ____ children.

2 a) Write down any words from this list which you think describe a good shepherd: reliable; kind; quick-tempered; watchful; calm; lazy; caring; understanding; thin; patient; loving.
   b) Which of these qualities are also useful for dealing with people? Give a reason for each answer.

3 a) Read the story about the black stone. Why was Muhammad's solution clever?
   b) Why do you think people did not resent him sliding the stone into place?
   c) Imagine you were one of the tribesmen arguing about the black stone. Next day, you meet a friend. Write down what you would tell them about the event. Make sure you include your *feelings* about what happened.

2 Muhammad's Message

One night, an angel appeared to Muhammad. 'Read,' he told Muhammad. But Muhammad could not read or write. Three times, Muhammad told the angel that he was not a reader; three times, the angel squeezed him hard. Then, the angel taught Muhammad this verse:

▶ Read in the name of your Lord who created.
Created man from a **clot** of blood.
Read, your Lord is most Generous.
Who taught by the pen.
Taught man what he did not know.   Qu'ran 96:1–5

On the way to Madinah, Muhammad spent the night in a cave. Soldiers from Makkah followed them but they did not look in the cave. This picture shows **Satan** leading them.

One of his wife's Christian relations told Muhammad he had seen God's messenger, the angel Gabriel. At first, Muhammad had been frightened. But his wife reassured him. She told him it was a sign that he had been chosen as a prophet.

Months later, he had another **vision** of the angel Gabriel. This really frightened Muhammad and he rushed home. Once again, his wife comforted him. This time, Muhammad made up his mind. God *had* chosen him as a prophet.

▶ O Khadijah, the time of slumber and rest is past. Gabriel has asked me to warn men and call them to Allah and to His worship. But whom shall I call? And who will listen to me?

So Muhammad began to preach that there was one God. The first people who listened were his wife and a young cousin. However, Muhammad's message slowly spread among the people in Makkah. Few people took it seriously.

The people of Makkah did not live good lives. Many of the men fought and were cruel to the women and children. They drank a lot. Above all, they worshipped **idols** – great stone statues in the city. The Ka'bah was used to house some of these idols; people danced round the Ka'bah to worship them.

Muhammad told them not to pray to these idols. His message was simple. There is only one God and he created the world. It was wicked to worship statues.

The merchants of Makkah were angry. Pilgrims came to visit their **pagan shrines**. It brought business into the city. They did not want Muhammad wrecking it. So they said he was a liar or a madman. Some of his followers were beaten up or tortured – and the attacks grew worse.

One day, pilgrims from the city of Yathrib heard Muhammad preach and were impressed. They invited him to go and live with them, over 400 km away across the Arabian desert. Muhammad accepted their invitation.

This is an important event for Muslims. They

THERE IS NO GOD BUT ALLAH AND MUHAMMAD IS HIS MESSENGER

Islam is like a house supported by five pillars. The first of these is the declaration of faith: 'There is no god but Allah and Muhammad is His Messenger'.

When this happens, God will judge us. Only God can judge and only God can forgive the wicked. People earn this forgiveness through prayers and actions.

▶ Actions shall be judged only by intention. A man shall get what he intends.

Sahih Al-Bukhari (Hadith)

The Will of God

God has created the world and, at all times, remains in control of the world. He has complete knowledge of what will happen in the world. However, people face many choices each day. They can do bad or they can do good. God expects people to make choices. So we are still responsible for our actions.

Life after Death

Those who obey God will go to Paradise. There, they will live forever a life of peace and happiness. Those who disobey God will go to Hell, where life will be miserable. Only God knows exactly what it is like in Paradise and Hell. Muhammad said there were things in Paradise which no eye has ever seen, no ear ever heard and no one can imagine.

▶ If anyone has got an **atom** of pride in his heart, he will not enter Paradise.

Sahih Al-Bukhari

1 Draw the diagram above. (You may miss out the Arabic writing, if you wish.) In later chapters, you will read about the other four pillars and can fill in the details.

2 a) Look at the painting of the angel. How is it shown?
b) Why do you think painters show angels like this?
c) If angels cannot be seen, why show them at all?

3 a) Think of an occasion when you did something you thought was wrong. Briefly, describe what you did.
b) What made you think it was wrong?
c) If you thought it was wrong, why did you do it?
d) Now, describe a time when you tried to do something good, but it went wrong.
e) Which of your two actions would a Muslim think was wrong? Explain how you decided.
f) Think back over the last week. Divide your page into two columns. Put a heading, MY BALANCE SHEET. In the left column, write down the good things you have done. On the right, write down the bad things.
g) Underneath, write a paragraph summing up your behaviour.

6 Prayer

Muslims believe that God has created human beings to worship Him. So the second pillar of Islam is prayer. Muslims must pray five times a day. Each time takes about ten minutes.

Men are asked to pray at mosques. However, if that is not possible, they may pray anywhere that is clean. Women are encouraged to pray at home. Every Muslim over the age of ten must perform these prayers. Children are taught to pray from the age of seven.

These five **compulsory** prayers are known as *Salat*. They help Muslims to remember God and keep them from doing bad deeds. Muslims must still pray if they are ill or even if they are fighting a war.

These five daily prayers do not mean that a Muslim cannot pray at other times. Other prayers, called *Du'ah*, may be made at any time, anywhere. But all Muslims are expected to say Salat. Once a week, on Fridays, there are special prayers at mid-day instead of the normal mid-day prayers.

All Muslims, wherever they are, face Makkah when they perform Salat. There is a special place in the mosque wall which shows them which way to face. Outside a mosque, some Muslims use a prayer mat with a compass in it.

This means that British Muslims face south-east when they pray. In Mexico, Muslims face east. In most of Africa, they face north-east.

▶ There's quite a lot of Muslim boys in our school. We have a separate room to pray in. Our headmaster is not **prejudiced**. One of the mothers asked him for a prayer room so they provided us with a special room. We only need to go there once for the afternoon prayer.   Darwa

▶ There's nowhere in my school where I can go. So, at the end of the day, I just put my prayers together.   Ali

1 Copy out this paragraph and fill in the gaps.
Muslims must pray _____ times a day. This is called _____ . When they do this, they face _____ . Other prayers are called _____ . These can be offered at any time.

2 a) Draw the diagram on this page.
b) Which prayer do you think is most inconvenient? Give reasons for your choice.
c) Why does Darwa only need the prayer room for the afternoon prayers?

3 a) Look at the picture strip on page 15. Why do you think Muslims must clean themselves before praying?
b) The following actions are all part of Salat. Write them down in the order in which they are done.
i)   Stand and face Makkah
ii)   Bow down with hands on knees
iii) Wash the face three times
iv)   Sit with knees bent
v)   Raise hands to ears
vi)   Wash both feet
vii) Clean the nostrils
viii) The call to prayer

4 In groups, write down reasons why a Muslim might want to say Du'ah. For instance, he or she might want to pray when a friend is ill. Afterwards, compare your answers.

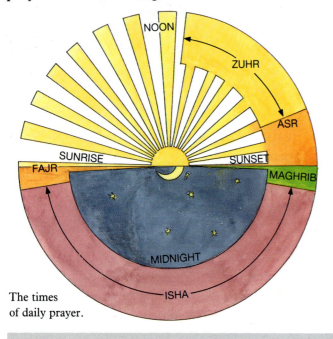

The times of daily prayer.

A Muslim must be clean. First, he performs Wudu (ablution). He says

IN THE NAME OF ALLAH THE MOST MERCIFUL, THE MOST KIND.

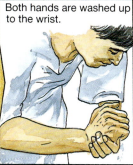

Both hands are washed up to the wrist.

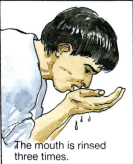

The mouth is rinsed three times.

The nostrils and tip of the nose are washed three times.

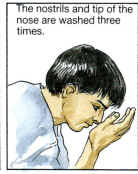

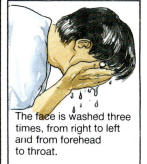

The face is washed three times, from right to left and from forehead to throat.

Each arm is washed three times.

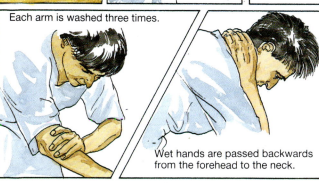

Wet hands are passed backwards from the forehead to the neck.

The ears and behind the ears are cleaned.

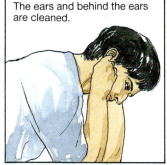

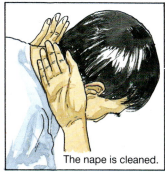

The nape is cleaned.

The feet are washed up to the ankles.

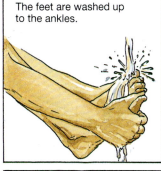

The Muslim says,

I BEAR WITNESS THAT THERE IS NO GOD BUT ALLAH AND I BEAR WITNESS THAT MUHAMMAD IS HIS SERVANT AND MESSENGER.

THE CALL TO PRAYER.

After the call to prayer, everyone faces the Ka'bah in Makkah.

Each Muslim says how many prayers he intends to say.

Women's positions are slightly different.

ALLAHU AKBAR

(Allah is the greatest)

O ALLAH, GLORY AND PRAISE ARE FOR YOU, AND BLESSED IS YOUR NAME, AND EXALTED IS YOUR MAJESTY; THERE IS NO GOD BUT YOU. I SEEK SHELTER IN ALLAH FROM THE REJECTED SATAN. IN THE NAME OF ALLAH, THE MOST MERCIFUL, THE MOST KIND.

He recites the opening chapter of the Qur'an and any one other chapter.

ALLAHU AKBAR. GLORY TO MY LORD, THE GREAT

(Three times)

ALLAH HEARS THOSE WHO PRAISE HIM. OUR LORD, PRAISE BE TO YOU.

ALLAHU AKBAR. GLORY TO MY LORD, THE HIGHEST.

(Three times)

ALLAHU AKBAR.

He rests a moment, then prostrates himself on the floor, repeating the words in the last picture.

Gets up, saying

ALLAHU AKBAR.

This ends one unit of salat.

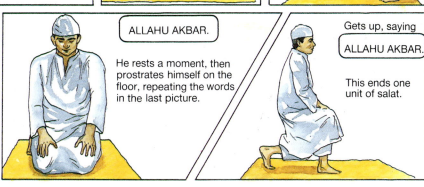

7 At the Mosque

Outside a mosque. Notice the fountain and the tall minarets.

Male Muslims offer their five daily prayers to God in special buildings called mosques. The word means 'place of **prostration**' because Muslims bow low to God when praying.

The very first mosque was built by Muhammad and his followers in Madinah. Today, there are thousands of mosques all over the world.

Most mosques have one or more tall slender towers called minarets. In Arab villages, a man in a turban stands on the balcony at the top. Facing towards the Ka'bah in Makkah, he calls other Muslims to prayer. He is called a muezzin. Today, a loudspeaker might be used instead but the same words are spoken in Arabic:

▶ Allah is the greatest
Allah is the greatest
Allah is the greatest
Allah is the greatest
I bear witness that there is no God but Allah
I bear witness that there is no God but Allah
I bear witness that Muhammad is Allah's messenger
I bear witness that Muhammad is Allah's messenger
Rush to prayer, rush to prayer,
Rush to success, rush to success,
Allah is the greatest
Allah is the greatest
There is no God but Allah

Every mosque must have somewhere for Muslims to wash themselves before going to pray. Larger mosques might have an open-air pool or a fountain; smaller ones might only offer cloakrooms. There must be space to leave shoes, too; Muslims always take them off before praying. It stops dust entering the holy building.

Inside, you would find the mosque very bare. There are no seats. People pray on their own mats or, in hot countries, they can use the cool floor. They stand in rows, shoulder to shoulder. It is a way of showing their brotherhood in their faith.

Muhammad had stopped people praying to idols. He was afraid that people might go back to worshipping them. So there are no paintings or statues in a mosque. Muslims are not allowed to draw animals or people – only God can create them.

These men are washing before they go into a mosque in Malaysia.

Inside a mosque. On the left, the mihrab, a **niche** showing the direction of the Ka'bah. On the right, the minbar where **sermons** are preached on Fridays.

Mosque walls may be decorated with patterns. Some are **mosaics**; others are drawn in plaster. There may be words as well; sentences taken from the Qur'an.

Often, only men go to the mosque. But, today, women attend services more than in the past. They stand separately from the men so that they don't distract each other. During prayers, Muslims are not allowed to touch someone of the opposite sex. In some Muslim countries, mosques have special areas for women.

This man came across a group of Muslims during his travels.

▶ As we walked along the hot, dusty road, we heard a strangely beautiful chant fill the air about us. Passing through a group of trees (we saw) on a high wooden tower, a blind Arab, in a white turban. The words which we did not understand fell upon our ears, Allahu Akbar, Allahu Akbar, La Ilaha illa 'i-Lah (there is no god but God).

Now we noticed that a great number of people were beginning to assemble. They spread long mats upon the ground. The people took off their shoes and sandals and formed long lines, one line falling in behind the other.

We were amazed that no distinctions of any kind were to be found in this **congregation**. Here were white men, yellow men, black men, poor men, wealthy men, beggars, and merchants, all standing side by side with no thought of race or social station in life. Not one single person looked away from the mat in front of him.

1 a) Write one sentence about each of these: mosque; minaret; minbar; mihrab; Ka'bah.
   b) Draw the picture of a mosque shown above. Write down what is shown at each of the numbered places.
2 Why do you think that:
   a) Muslims wash before praying?
   b) Muslims take off their shoes?
   c) They don't look at other people?
   d) They stand shoulder to shoulder?
3 Read the quotation on this page.
   a) What was the blind Arab doing?
   b) What were these Muslims about to do?
   c) Why do you think they took off their shoes when they were outside?
   d) What most impressed him about this sight?
4 What do you think a Muslim would do if:
   a) No water was available?
   b) He was in an aeroplane at the time for Salat?
   c) He was too ill to get to a mosque?
   d) He was late for the service?

8 Imams

His day is spent showing school groups and other visitors round the mosque. There are talks to prepare and letters to answer. People write to him to find out about Islam. In the evening, there are more prayers to lead. Abdul Jalid Sajid is an imam in Brighton. He is also kept very busy:

▶ I organise many activities; educational and religious programmes at the mosque, financial and building projects, an Islamic school for children each evening and midweek classes for other groups. I visit many schools in the area, and speak to many non-Muslim groups. I am also the Muslim prison and hospital **chaplain** for Sussex.

Regent's Park Mosque.

There are no priests in Islam. Each person is his own priest. But Muslims do have religious leaders, called imams. These people are chosen because they have much religious knowledge and because people know them to be good Muslims.

These imams are not usually paid for doing the job. They do the work in their spare time. They earn their money by doing another full-time job. However, in a big mosque, they may get paid for being a secretary or caretaker.

Shaikh Gamal Solaiman is imam at the Regent's Park mosque in London. He described some of his work.

▶ An Imam does a lot of things. In addition to sermons, advising people, leading the prayer and so on, he is also busy with other aspects of care. He contacts and visits **bereaved** people, sick people and sometimes people in prison. I start very early and end very late.

The imam's day begins with morning prayer, which can be as early as 3.00 am. Afterwards, he will read the Qur'an. Only then does he have breakfast and perhaps rest before his day's work starts.

This imam is studying the Qur'an at a mosque in Egypt. The large object is a fan.

A mosque usually has a school for young Muslims, called a *madressa*. This one is at Kano in Nigeria.

Many mosques run schools where Muslim children learn about their religion. They are taught to read Arabic so they can learn the Qur'an. Some mosques run these lessons daily. Children go to them after their day's work at school. The Regent's Park mosque is different. The imam explained:

▶ We receive them only one day a week, at weekends. The facilities are limited. I personally think, although three to four hours a week is not enough, coming to the mosque at the end of a very long school day would be a bit much. We are just trying to strike some middle way – neither to overburden the children nor to neglect them.

But Fridays are special. The Arabic word for Friday means *Day of Assembly*. Instead of the usual noon prayers, a special act of worship takes place. All adult men must take part. Women are allowed to join in as long as it does not interfere with their work at home. If there is no mosque locally, the prayers can be said anywhere – in a park or on a farm, for instance.

One part of Friday prayer is a khutbah (sermon) given by the imam. It has two parts. In the first part, he will recite from the Qur'an, then explain what it means. In the second part, he will pray for all Muslims everywhere.

But the sermon goes beyond this. The Friday prayer brings all Muslims in a community together. So the imam may use the occasion to talk about any current events which affect Muslims.

Afterwards, the congregation may discuss local problems. Then everyone goes back to work. Friday is not a day of rest for Muslims, as Sunday is for Christians.

1 Match up the words on the left with the meanings on the right.

imam	Muslims' holy book
khutbah	Muslims' Day of Assembly
Friday	sermon
madressa	Muslim religious leader
Qur'an	mosque school

2 a) Why do you think a Muslim would agree to become an imam?
b) Which of the following words do you think would describe a good imam? (Give reasons for your choices.) unfriendly; helpful; kind; lonely; cheerful; solitary; serious; religious; caring; hopeful.

3 a) Two imams are described in this chapter. Which jobs are done by both of them?
b) Which job do you think an imam would see as most important? Explain how you decided.

4 a) How are the Islamic schools in Brighton and London different?
b) Why does the London mosque hold school only on Saturdays?
c) Do you think it is better for the children to attend every day or not? Give reasons for your view.

5 Suppose a new mosque has opened near where you live but they do not have an imam. Make up an advert or a poster to get someone to do the job. Your answers to 2(b) may give you ideas.

9 Zakat (alms)

▶ He is a not believer who eats his fill while his neighbour remains hungry by his side.
the Hadith

Muslims believe that everything people have has been given by God. More than that, everything we have *belongs* to God. And that includes our money and possessions.

Strictly speaking, these things are not ours, they are God's. So we should use them as he wishes them to be used. We should spend our money in ways he will approve of. This means giving things to those who need them, not keeping all our money for ourselves.

Muslims believe that poor people have a right to share in the wealth of the rich people. Zakat is a kind of tax which makes sure this happens. It is the third pillar of Islam.

Every Muslim has a duty to pay Zakat. Each year, well-off Muslims must give some of their wealth away. It will be used for good causes or to help the poor. Muslims believe it is a sin to let people suffer from hunger or disease. They also think that hanging on to all your wealth is greedy. That, too, is a sin.

The amount to be paid varies. Every Muslim who has money left at the end of the year has to give at least 2.5% (one fortieth) of it away. Farmers must give at least 5% of their crops and a number of animals. Traders give 2.5% of the value of their goods.

Islamic governments take the money from Muslims and share it amongst the needy. If a Muslim lives in a country which isn't Islamic (such as Britain) then Islamic organisations collect and distribute it.

A Muslim can give Zakat direct to another person if he or she wishes. But Muslims believe it is better to give secretly. That way, the giver will not feel proud and the poorer person will not be embarrassed. Muhammad himself said:

▶ The best charity is that which the right hand gives and the left hand does not know of it.

1. THE POOR AND NEEDY
2. PEOPLE WHO HAVE RECENTLY BECOME MUSLIMS
4. PEOPLE IN DEBT
3. PRISONERS-OF-WAR
5. MUSLIM TAX-COLLECTORS (FOR WAGES)
6. MUSLIMS STUDYING ISLAM
8. HOSPITALS, SCHOOLS, LIBRARIES AND MOSQUES
7. TRAVELLERS WHO NEED HELP

The Qur'an lays down who may receive Zakat.

These men are paying Zakat as they enter a mosque in North Africa. Notice the Arabic writing and the mosaic patterns on the walls.

Zakat is an act of worship. It is not charity, like giving money on a flag day. It is a duty. It gives to others the wealth that should be theirs.

Nor should people who pay it feel proud. If they were proud of giving the money, they would feel superior to those who receive it. But Muslims believe that everyone is equal. Zakat helps to make a fairer society.

A British imam explained how Zakat works:

▶ We collect our charity between ourselves. (Then) we seek out any Muslim, for instance a mother whose husband has died and she has several children. Although she gets money from the government, it is still not enough to buy clothes for her children.

But it is left to the conscience of the Muslim. There is nobody coming around asking, 'How much do you earn? How much have you got in the bank?' It is left to your conscience because it is an obligation. If you cheat, which you can do, you're not cheating anybody. You're cheating yourself because you will have to answer on the Day of Reckoning to God why you were so stingy, why you were so mean, why you didn't pay your charity out of the money that God has provided you with.

1 Answer these questions in complete sentences:
a) What is Zakat?
b) Why must Muslims pay Zakat?
c) How is Zakat organised in an Islamic country?
d) How is it done in Britain?

2 a) In groups, look at the drawing on page 20. Write down why each of these people might need help: (a) a traveller abroad, (b) people who have just become Muslims, (c) prisoners-of-war, (d) Muslims studying Islam.
b) Which of the eight groups would you prefer your Zakat to go to? Give reasons for your choice.

3 a) Why is it a good idea to be told to help the poor?
b) Can you think of any disadvantages of the idea?

4 a) Muslims believe in an equal society. In pairs, discuss whether you think Britain is an equal society. Write down any ways you think it is or is not equal.
b) Then, write down ways in which you could make a society equal.
c) As a class, compare your answers. Are they better or worse than paying Zakat?

10 Sawm (fasting)

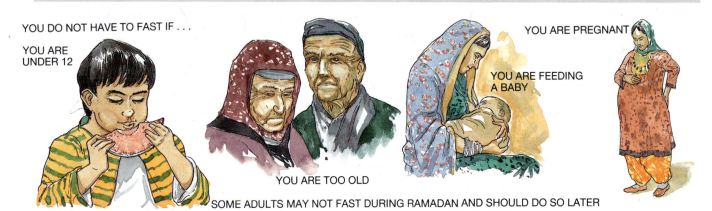

YOU DO NOT HAVE TO FAST IF . . .

YOU ARE UNDER 12

YOU ARE TOO OLD

YOU ARE PREGNANT

YOU ARE FEEDING A BABY

SOME ADULTS MAY NOT FAST DURING RAMADAN AND SHOULD DO SO LATER

This is the fourth pillar of Islam. It lays down that, at certain times, Muslims must fast – in other words, not eat.

Just like Zakat, Sawm is an act of worship. Muslims accept they may have to suffer in order to obey God. They know they must accept God's commands at all times. Sawm helps them to remember this.

Fasting helps a Muslim to appreciate how the poor suffer. It is a kind of training which makes it easier for Muslims to be obedient. It also brings Muslims together because they all fast at the same time.

The fasting takes place during the ninth month of the Islamic calendar. The month is called *Ramadan*. One African tribe calls it the 'thirst month'. This was the month when the Qur'an was revealed to Muhammad.

Islamic months are based on the moon and move forward by ten or eleven days each year. The fast lasts for 29 or 30 days (depending on when the new moon is first seen).

All adult Muslims go without food from just before dawn until just after sunset. Even chewing is not allowed. They do not drink, smoke or make love, either. Children under about twelve do not have to take part. However, young children are encouraged to fast for a day or two in the month. Two Muslim boys described what fasting is like:

▶ You feel the need of the poor and hungry. You're only fasting for a day. You're going to eat food at sunset. But they feel hungry all the time.

There are also medical benefits. More than half of the cases of heart diseases are due to overweight so by fasting you slim yourself. But if you fast just to slim yourself, you're just wasting your time. You fast because you'll get rewarded in life after death.

In the beginning you feel hungry but then you get used to it. I went to school and I played athletics although I was fasting. I didn't feel anything because I got used to it.

▶ You start feeling a bit hungry about four o'clock. But if you start feeling hungry, you read the Qur'an.

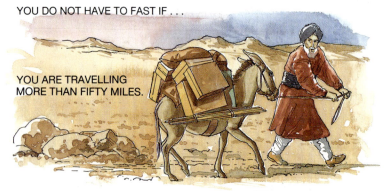

YOU DO NOT HAVE TO FAST IF . . .

YOU ARE TRAVELLING MORE THAN FIFTY MILES.

YOU ARE SICK

SICK MUSLIMS MAY FEED A HUNGRY PERSON FOR EACH DAY THEY DO NOT FAST.

The first meal after sunset. Muhammad broke his fast with a meal of dates and water. Many Muslims still do this today. A popular drink is made from dried apricots, which are high in glucose.

Muslims usually have a meal just before dawn during the month of Ramadan. Even so, going without food all day is not easy, no matter how old a person is. It might seem tempting to hide somewhere and have a quick snack. But Muslims know that this cheating may fool other people, but it won't fool God. God can see them all the time.

> ▶ I can't eat a lot early in the morning, but it is beneficial to have a light breakfast. But it's mainly the drink that's important to sustain yourself for the rest of the day. Normally, I return to bed some time after 4.30 (a.m.) and sleep through until I have to get up to work in the morning.
> It does make the well-to-do section of society more aware of the suffering of other human beings in the world who do not have the means to have one good meal a day.   Zahid Khan

Muslims are also very careful not to do any bad actions during their fast. No Muslim should tell a lie or break a promise during the whole month.

Each night during Ramadan, Muslims say special prayers. If they can do this in a mosque, they should do so. These prayers involve speaking and listening to as much of the Qur'an as possible. Ideally, Muslims should finish the whole book during Ramadan.

One night is specially important during the month. This is Lailat ul Qadr (the Night of Power). The Qur'an was revealed to Muhammad on this night. By tradition, it is celebrated on an odd-numbered day during the last ten nights of Ramadan. On this night, Muslims should try to stay awake and offer special prayers.

1 Match up the words on the left with the correct meaning on the right.
Ramadan   Muslims' holy book
Sawm   Islamic ninth month
Lailat ul Qadr   fasting
Qur'an   the Night of Power
2 a) Why do you think these people do not fast during Ramadan: children; sick people; pregnant mothers?
b) What are the benefits of fasting?
c) Why does the boy think it's useless to fast if you're just trying to lose weight?
d) Why do you think the other boy reads the Qur'an when he starts to feel hungry?
e) What would you do if you started to feel hungry? Explain your answer.
3 a) Do you think it's easier to fast in summer or winter? Give reasons.
b) What would be the problems of fasting in (i) Africa and (ii) Greenland?

II *Hajj (pilgrimage)*

Each day all Muslims turn during prayer towards the Ka'bah in Makkah. Once in a lifetime, each Muslim is expected to travel to Makkah, as long as he or she can afford to go. This pilgrimage is called the hajj. It is the final pillar of Islam.

The Ka'bah is seen by Muslims as God's house. They believe it was first built by Adam and later rebuilt by the prophet Abraham and his son Ishmael. It is a simple cube-shaped building, covered with black cloth. But Muslims believe it was the first place ever built just for the worship of God.

Each year, during the twelfth Islamic month, two million Muslims from all over the world go to Makkah. Non-Muslims are not allowed into the city.

The hajj reminds Muslims that they are all equal in the eyes of God. So, as they near Makkah, the pilgrims change their clothes. Instead of ordinary clothes, a male Muslim wears two sheets of unsewn white cloth. Women may wear their everyday clothes, but must be covered from head to ankles.

The white sheets are **symbolic**. They remind Muslims that they must be willing to give up everything for God. It is also a reminder that dead people are wrapped in similar sheets. After death, all fine clothes and wealth are of no value.

The hajj lasts five days. In that time, each Muslim is expected to think of God constantly. On the first day, the pilgrimage begins at Makkah. Each Muslim walks seven times around the Ka'bah, starting at the black stone. Some pilgrims try to kiss it, as a sign of respect.

Next, the pilgrim goes to two small hills nearby. Here, God ordered Abraham to leave his wife Hagar and son Ishmael. When their water supply ran out, Hagar ran up and down the hills. She was desperately looking for water. Today's pilgrims walk briskly backwards and forwards in memory of her search.

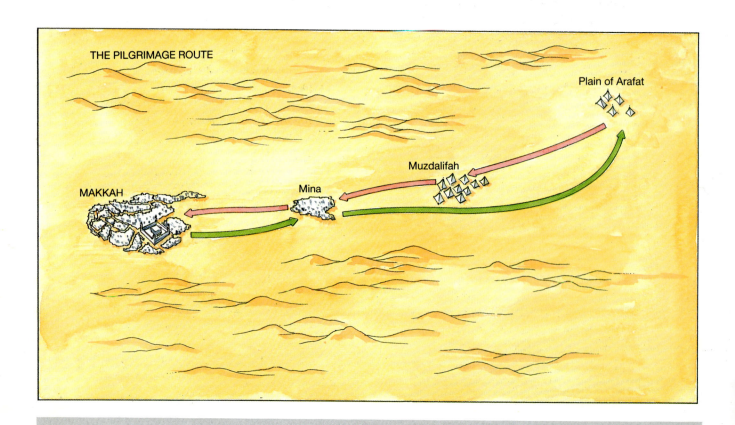

THE PILGRIMAGE ROUTE

Plain of Arafat

Muzdalifah

Mina

MAKKAH

The decorations on this house show that the owner has been on the hajj. Such a man is called a hajji; a woman is called a hajja.

The pilgrims spend the night at Mina. At sunrise on the following day, they go to the valley of Arafat. Thousands of tents are put up specially to protect the pilgrims from the heat. Here, they spend the day meditating in the sun. After sunset, they all leave to spend the night at Muzdalifah. Part of the evening is spent hunting for 49 small stones for the next part of the hajj.

Returning to Mina, they set off for three stone pillars. These mark the places where the devil tried to get Ishmael to disobey Abraham. Muslims believe that Ishmael drove the devil away by throwing stones at him. So modern Muslims throw their stones at these pillars. It is a way of showing that they reject evil and wish to follow God.

The pilgrimage ends with a festival. Animals are **sacrificed**. Abraham had been willing to sacrifice his son on God's command. When God spared Ishmael, Abraham sacrificed a ram instead.

So modern pilgrims sacrifice a sheep, goat, cow or camel. This is a symbol of how willing they are to give up their lives and possessions for God. Pilgrims eat some of the meat; much of it is given to the poor. Afterwards, they circle the Ka'bah once more; many go on afterwards to Madinah.

All Muslims are expected to go on the hajj at least once in their lifetime if they can afford to do so. However, if they are too sick, they may get someone else to go on their behalf. Many Muslims actually go more than once. It is a great occasion in their lives.

One hajji explained what the pilgrimage was like.

▶ You find yourself moved and touched. You have become a very small part of a great assembly. Sometimes, you don't worry about the details of the order of events. In fact, the Prophet himself was doing his favourite pilgrimage and certain people came up to him and said, 'I did this before that'. Sometimes, they would say, 'I threw the stone before I shaved' or 'I ordered my sacrifice before I did it.'

All the time, he'd say, 'Do the rest and there is no blame attached.' It is good to know what steps to do but, as far as feeling them, that can only be obtained by going there. It is an amazing experience.

1 a) Write down one thing which each of these people did in or around Makkah: (i) Abraham; (ii) Hagar; (iii) Ishmael.
  b) For each event, write down what modern Muslims do to remember them.
2 a) Put these events from the hajj in the order in which they happen:
  i)   Stoning the pillars at Mina
  ii) Putting on ihram (pilgrims' clothes)
  iii) Sacrificing an animal
  iv) Spending the day at Arafat
  v)   Walking between the two hills
  vi) Going seven times round the Ka'bah
  b) Write down one event which is missing from your list.
3 a) Read the quotation above. How does it add to your understanding of the hajj?
  b) Why did this hajji find it 'an amazing experience'?

It is the custom for Muslim babies' heads to be shaved.

Birth

If a child has Muslim parents, it is considered to be a Muslim at birth. But children are a gift from God. So the parents are honoured that He should give them a new life.

The first words a Muslim baby hears are the call to prayer in Arabic (printed on page 16). This is called the Adhan and is spoken into the baby's right ear. Immediately afterwards, another prayer (Iqamah) is whispered in its left ear.

Back from hospital, dates or honey are placed in the baby's mouth. Muslims pray that the child may have a sweet, trouble-free life. However, the main ceremony comes seven days after the birth. This is called aqiqah.

First, the child's head is shaved of all its hair. In theory, gold or silver equal to the weight of this hair is then given to the poor. But it depends how well-off the family is. Sometimes, much more is given. Today, current money (like £5 notes) can be given instead.

Next, the baby gets its name. This may be one of the ninety-nine names of God. If not, it could be a prophet's name or the name of someone in Muhammad's family.

Afterwards, friends and neighbours come for a meal. Usually, a lamb or a goat will have been killed. However, if the family is poor, it might be a chicken. Whatever it is, some of the food will be given to the poor. This is what happens at one British mosque.

▶ The father will bring the food and will invite everybody in the mosque to join. Usually, everybody present in the mosque will go and attend. Naturally, there will be many people. Poverty is relative. There may not be many people here as poor as in Bangladesh.

As soon as possible, the child will begin learning Arabic letters so that he or she can read the Qur'an. At first, the child listens to an adult reading the Qur'an, then repeats it word by word. As soon as possible, he or she will be learning parts of the book by heart.

Death

Death is always an occasion for sadness. But a dying Muslim may feel a kind of happiness. All Muslims believe in a life after death. And, on the Day of Judgment, loved ones will meet again.

A Muslim who knows he is about to die will repeat: 'There is no God but Allah, and Muhammad is his messenger.' After death, the body will be washed and wrapped in a white cloth – three for a man, five for a woman. If the dead person has made the hajj to Makkah, the

Muslim funeral customs vary from one country to another. This funeral is taking place in Pakistan, but the Muslims have come from neighbouring Afghanistan.

body will be wrapped in the white pilgrim's clothes.

▶ If the law requires people to be buried in a coffin, the religious teaching is to respect such a law. I think how a person is buried is a matter of custom, rather than religious law. What is necessary is to maintain the dignity of death. The body should not be cremated, broken or left exposed.

The burial takes place as soon as possible. Cremation is forbidden. Muslims try to bury their dead so that their head is facing towards the Ka'bah. As the earth is put over the body, people recite from the Qur'an: 'We created you from it and deposit you into it and from it will take you out once more.'

Seven days after the burial, relatives often go back to the grave. It is a mark of respect. Of course, the relatives are sad but they remember the words of Muhammad. He taught that a good Muslim will have left behind three great gifts for others. The first of these is money; the second is knowledge; the third is the example which he has given his children. They, too, will grow as Muslims and praise God. For that, they will always have the dead person to thank.

1 a) Islam teaches Muslims to care for the poor. What actions in this chapter help the poor?
b) Muslims are not allowed expensive gravestones. Why do you think that is?
c) Do you think it would be better if no one had gravestones? Explain your answer.
2 a) What three gifts may a dead Muslim leave behind?
b) Who could benefit from each of these? (Three different answers.)
c) Which do you think is the most important of these gifts? Give a reason for your choice.
d) Think of someone you respect. Do you think that person would be pleased with how you live your life? Explain your answer.

13 Getting Married

► O mankind, be mindful of your duty to your Lord who created you from a single soul and from it created its mate and from the two created many men and women.

Qur'an 4:1

Marriage is very important to Muslims. Most of the prophets, including Muhammad, were married. Muslims believe that the Qur'an tells them that they should get married: it is a religious duty.

This applies to both men and women. Islam gives equal rights to men and women. In fact, a Muslim wife keeps her own name after marriage; also, any property she owned before the marriage remains hers. And her husband must provide her with whatever help she was used to having before marriage.

What makes Muslim marriages different to most western marriages is that the parents try to find a suitable bride or groom. Sometimes, the boy and girl do not even meet until after the parents have agreed. This is known as an arranged marriage. Love comes after the couple get married, not before.

MW916: Thirty-one year old Moroccan computer student, kind natured, seeks equally pious Muslima for future life together.

MW911: Scottish Muslim, forty-two years young, qualified psychiatric nurse, 5ft. 7ins., likes writing, seeks suitable lifelong partner.

Advertisements like these are placed in newspapers and magazines by Muslim parents.

This does not mean the couple has no say in the matter. Both partners must agree before the marriage goes ahead. However, most youngsters

Muslim marriage ceremonies vary around the world. They are organised according to each country's laws and customs. This photo shows the wedding of a princess in Morocco.

A Muslim bridegroom signs the marriage contract. This is the one thing that must happen in every Muslim marriage. The details of this contract will have been agreed by the couple and their families.

seem to trust their parents to make these choices for them. Muslims believe that married people know best what is needed for a good marriage. This Muslim woman describes how her marriage was arranged:

▶ I was just about to go to Birmingham to start my law degree but my mother felt that for a girl of nineteen to go away from home for the first time . . . was unacceptable. She felt that I had to be married. She felt that marriage would provide a kind of barrier round me, saying, 'Keep off. Married.'

So I was married. It was an arranged marriage, as is (normal) in many Asian families. I knew my husband beforehand. I knew his **temperament** and we got on pretty well anyway.

The two sets of parents will fix the marriage contract. This includes a dowry. This is money given by the man to his future wife. It shows that she is needed and that the man will be responsible for her. Sometimes, part of this is paid before the wedding to help the woman get ready for her marriage. The rest is usually only paid if the couple split up.

This does not happen often. Muslims are allowed to divorce but it is not encouraged.

Rather, the couple are encouraged to sort out their problems first. Divorce is so rare among Muslims that it is not a problem.

Muslim weddings are simple affairs although everyone wears their very best clothes. The marriage can take place at a mosque or at the bride's home. Two witnesses must be present. There may be a reading from the Qur'an and sweets are shared out. The next day, the bridegroom gives a feast for all their relatives and friends.

Muslim men are allowed to marry more than one wife. They may have up to four. But this is rare. Muhammad said that a man must treat each wife equally and very few Muslims can afford to do this. It may happen if the first wife is unable to have children. However, it is not done in countries such as Tunisia and Britain, where it is against the law.

1 Answer these questions in complete sentences:
   a) What is an arranged marriage?
   b) What is a dowry and who pays it?
   c) Why is it rare for a Muslim to have more than one wife?
   d) Where do Muslim marriages take place?
   e) What is Muslims' attitude to divorce?
   f) What evidence is there that husbands and wives have equal treatment?
2 a) How do you think Muslim parents would go about choosing a bride or groom?
   b) List (i) the advantages and (ii) the disadvantages of letting your parents make the choice.
3 a) Who will choose the person you marry?
   b) How will the person in (a) make this choice? Answer in detail.
   c) Does this mean the marriage will be a success? Give reasons.
   d) If Muslim divorces are rare, does this mean that arranged marriages are successful? Explain your answer carefully.
4 As a class, compare your answers to 2(b). Which is the longer list?

14 Family Life

Muslims believe that family life is essential for a healthy society. So the Qur'an lays down very clear guidelines for family life. No child, it says, should cause harm to his or her parents. They should be loved and cared for. This conversation took place between a man and Muhammad.

> ▶ Man: Who deserves the best care from me?
> Muhammad: Your mother.
> Man: Who else after that?
> Muhammad: Your mother.
> Man: Who else?
> Muhammad: Your mother.
> Man: Then who else?
> Muhammad: Your father.

As they grow older, parents may need to be supported by the children. This may mean actually having the parents living with them or helping them out with money. This duty continues until the parents' deaths.

Above all, parents may expect their children to obey them. So family ties in Muslim families are often stronger than those in non-Muslim families. Obedience is a duty, partly in return for what the parents have done for the children in the past.

This Muslim family, from the Near East, wears mainly western-style clothes.

> ▶ Your Lord has ordered that you worship none but Him and [show] kindness to your parents. Whether either of them or both of them attain old age in your life, never say to them, 'Ough' nor be harsh with them, but speak to them kindly.
> And serve them with tenderness and **humility** and say, 'My Lord, have mercy on them, just as they cared for me as a little child.'
>
> Qur'an 17:23–24

However, parents are not always right. The Qur'an gives a number of examples of parents making mistakes. So children should also be aware of what God wishes. If there is a conflict, the child should do as God would wish.

Muslim girls and boys are expected to work hard at school and do well. Muslims believe that education makes good human beings. As a result, Muslims tend to be very law-abiding. An imam said this:

> ▶ The Qur'an requires children to respect their parents and be kind to them. The Prophet says if your parents are angry with you, this may bring you the anger of God as well. So it is always hammered, especially in western countries, with the sense of freedom here.

This Malaysian family follows the Muslim practice of washing before and after meals.

In many Muslim countries, the extended family is common, as in this Iraqi family.

Muslim parents tend to be strict with their children. They are not encouraged to go to parties; mixed dancing is not allowed. Their parents will not approve of boyfriends and girlfriends. Sex outside marriage is forbidden.

These rules can cause problems for Muslims living in a non-Muslim country, such as Britain. Muslim teenagers see other teenagers going to discos and wearing western clothes. They might want to copy this. This can start arguments between parents and children.

But parents, too, have duties. Muhammad said that people who are kindest to their families show the most perfect faith. He himself was fond of children; he believed that Muslims would become known for their kindness to children.

▶ Parents have to set an example. That is one of the functions of the **extended family**, when three generations are living together. The grandchild will see how his father is treating his father. Of course, I can't say all children are obedient and respectful to their parents. But I think that Muslims are more fortunate than others.
Shaikh Gamal Solaiman

The Qur'an makes it clear that every child has a right to be treated equally. No parent should ever harm their own child. If the parents are dead, the nearest relatives must care for the **orphan**. If there are no relatives, then other Muslims should take on this task.

1 a) Write down two duties which Muslim children owe their parents.
b) Do you think these are good rules to live by? Give reasons.
c) Write down two duties which Muslim parents owe their children.
d) Do you think these are good rules to live by? Give reasons.
2 a) How do Muslim children show respect for their parents?
b) How do you show respect for yours? (If you don't, say why.)
c) Think carefully! How can parents show respect for children?
3 a) Which of the following do you think your parents would like you to be when you grow up: honest; kind; successful; rich; happy; popular; religious; truthful; trusting; a loving parent; hard-working?
b) Write down the two things you would most like to be. Explain how you chose them.
c) For non-Muslims only! Do you think a Muslim would have written the same? Explain your answer.
d) As a group, compare your answers to (b). What do you notice about the differences?

15 *Muslim Women*

These Muslim women, outside a mosque in Old Delhi, have their faces covered.

Many western people think that Muslim women do not get equal treatment with men. In fact, the aim of Islam is quite the opposite.

At the time of Muhammad, pagan Arabs saw women as possessions to be bought and sold. Islam, on the other hand, gave women an important place. They were to be honoured and respected. 'Paradise,' said Muhammad, 'lies at the feet of your mothers.'

Muslim women's rights are equal to those of men. Muslims believe that God created all people equal – but not **identical**. Men and women, they argue, have different qualities.

Their duties are different. Muslim men's duties are work and public affairs. A Muslim woman's main duties are to look after the home and care for her family. This does not mean that a Muslim woman may not work outside her home. Many Muslim women are nurses, teachers or doctors. In farming villages, Muslim men and women share the work.

▶ During the time of the Prophet, the women worked, the women [took part] in wars. According to the Qur'an, I can see no problem. The women are allowed to work and they should **participate** in life. They have equal legal rights and equal obligations. This is what Islam gives the woman in theory. In practice, you find it quite different.

Egyptian woman

In fact, a Muslim woman's freedom mainly depends on which country she lives in. And this freedom can change, depending on who rules the country.

In Saudi Arabia, women are not allowed to drive cars. Yet many go to university and go on to do important jobs. There is even a women's bank, run by women for women customers only. Even so, most Saudi women lead their lives entirely inside the family circle. Very few women go out to work.

Wahda Ahmed Mesoud is the first female police officer in Oman. As a Muslim, she goes on duty in the long skirt she is wearing here.

▶ Bedouin men see their women as flowers blazing in the deserts. They dress them up in bright colours, just like flowers. Women are their poetry, their music, their joy – what gives meaning to their [lives]. All this is much more important to both women and men that what the world so often sees as limitations on women's lives.

At home, it is the women who take most of the important decisions. It is the women who decide what jobs the men will take, how the men will spend the money, what the children will do, whom they will marry.

In any case, Muslims themselves disagree about how much freedom a woman should have. Some Muslims look at the high divorce rates of western Europe and are worried that family life is falling apart. They believe that abortions and schoolgirl pregnancies show what happens when young people have too much freedom.

Others say that women play an important part in bringing up the next generation. So they should be involved in public life, where decisions are made which will affect their children.

This British Muslim woman gives another reason:

▶ How on earth can we go to a hospital and say, 'I want a Muslim woman doctor, one who I can speak to in my own language'? How on earth can we ask for this if we ourselves are not prepared to go out and educate ourselves so that we can become these things?

Bedouin women in the desert. Honour is very important to them. They would not talk to strange men.

1 a) On your own, write down the ways in which you think men and women are equal.
b) Now, write down any ways in which you think they are not equal.
c) In groups, discuss your answers. You will need one person who will report to the class about the group's answers. So you need to try and reach agreement.
d) Look at the photograph at the top of page 32. Do you think wearing veils means that these women are not being treated equally?
e) Still in groups, do you think Muslim women are equal or not? Be ready with reasons.

2 You need some daily newspapers for this question.
a) In groups, go through them and try to find examples of unequal treatment of women. Stick your item in your exercise book and explain how it shows that women are not equal.
b) Now, look for an example of a woman being exploited. Describe the item and write down how the woman is being exploited.
c) Which of your examples would Muslims disapprove of? Explain how you decided.

16 Muslim Festivals

These Indonesian Muslims are about to enjoy an Eid meal.

Islam, like all other world religions, has its festivals. Each is called *Eid*, which means festival. They are events of great joy for Muslims all over the world. But they are not held purely for fun and enjoyment. They are duties, to give thanks to God.

Eid ul-Fitr comes at the end of Ramadan. Muslims thank God for the Qur'an and for helping them to fast throughout the month. (If necessary, they will ask his forgiveness for any failures.)

In Muslim countries, Eid ul-Fitr is a national holiday. Muslims visit friends and relations, wearing their best clothes. The well-off give to the poor so that they, too, may enjoy the day. Everyone eats special food and the children are given presents. This Muslim boy gave his view of Eid ul-Fitr.

► We do what is prescribed for us. We take it as it comes as part of life. As kids, in Ramadan, you come to the mosque and get a chance to meet your friends. At Eid, everybody gives each other presents. That's probably the favourite festival.

Above all, Eid is a time for prayer. The festival begins with prayers at the mosque. Unlike festivals in other religions, Muslims do not dance or go to discos; they do not go to parties. It is more a time for the family to get together; a chance to meet your neighbours.

Eid ul-Fitr was begun by Muhammad himself. So was the second major festival, Eid ul-Adha. (It means festival of sacrifice.) This festival remembers the time when Abraham was ready to sacrifice Ishmael because God commanded it. By taking part, modern Muslims are showing that they, too, are ready to sacrifice their lives for God.

Eid ul-Adha comes towards the end of the hajj. It also begins with prayers at the mosque. This day, too, is a public holiday in Muslim countries. Even in non-Muslim countries, many Muslims take a day off to celebrate.

They sacrifice an animal, just as God eventually told Abraham to sacrifice a sheep. So the event is symbolic. God does not want the animal (or its meat); God wants Muslims to show him their **devotion**. The meat itself is shared with friends and relatives and, of course, the poor.

These Kenyan boys are dancing to celebrate Muhammad's birthday on 12th Rabi ul-Awwal.

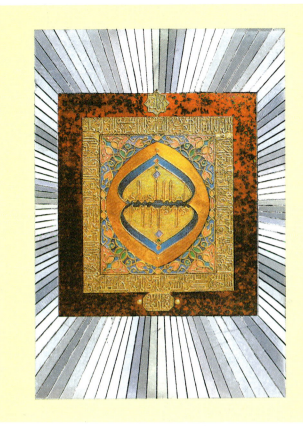

Eid card. These are sent to friends and relatives at Eid ul-Fitr. The cover often has a beautiful and detailed design.

A British Muslim describes Eid ul-Adha:

▶ My feelings were feelings of joy. It was a day to celebrate a great occasion that had taken place hundreds of years ago in the Mounts of Arafat. It was a day when I could ask for forgiveness. It was a day when I could join hundreds of other people who were worshipping their creator. It was a day when I am convinced that my prayers are answered.

Apart from these two major festivals, Muslims also celebrate four events in Muhammad's life. Strictly speaking, they are not festivals. But most Muslims remember them.

Lailat ul-Qadr has already been mentioned. This remembers the night when Muhammad was first given the words of the Qur'an. Muslims spend the night in prayer, reading from the Qur'an.

Ashura, on the 10th Muharram, reminds Muslims of the day when Noah left his ark and Moses saved the Israelites from the Egyptians. Muslims fast for two days. Another festival is mentioned in the lower caption on page 34.

With best wishes on the occasion of Eid.

We pray Allah Subhana Wa ta Ala to bless you and the Islamic Ummah with His unbounded Grace.

An Eid greeting.

1 Match up the events in list A with what they celebrate in list B.
List A: Eid ul-Fitr; Eid ul-Adha; Lailat ul-Qadr; Ashura; 12th Rabi ul-Awwal.
List B: Muhammad's birthday; Noah leaving the ark; Festival of Sacrifice; the end of fasting; the night of power.
2 Why do you think:
a) Muslims wear special clothes for Eid ul-Fitr?
b) They do not go to parties or discos on this occasion?
c) Muslims remember Muhammad's birthday?
d) The Eid card has no people drawn on it?
e) The Muslim is sure his prayers are answered at Eid ul-Adha?
3 Look at the Eid card shown above. Notice the vivid colours. Design your own card to send a friend. Remember that there will be no pictures of people on it. If you draw it on a piece of card, you could copy the Arabic writing on to the back of it.

The Qur'an gives all the guidance Muslims need on how to run their lives. Apart from daily prayers, Muslims are expected to read the Qur'an regularly. It teaches people how to create a fair society. In Islam, all people are equal. No one is a second-class citizen because of the colour of their skin – or for any other reason.

The Qur'an goes into more detail on daily life than the holy books of some other religions. Some Muslim countries base their laws on those of the Qur'an. For instance, it tells business-people how to run their businesses. It even tells them which businesses they may not run.

No Muslim is allowed to earn a living from gambling or alcohol. Islam bans both these things. No Muslim should earn a living by crime. Muslims must not earn a living from doing anything which harms society. Indeed,

These Muslim boys are holding prayer boards.

Muslims are some of the most law-abiding people in the world.

Muslim business people must be fair and honest. They may loan money to other people. But they are not allowed to charge **interest** on it. Islam teaches Muslims that the rich should help the poor. Paying interest means the poor are giving money to the rich. This does not mean that Muslims cannot make a profit. In fact, Muslims run very many successful businesses throughout the world.

The Qur'an also gives advice about clothing. Islam does not force Muslims to wear any particular kind of clothes. But Muslims believe that people are the best of God's creatures. So their dress should always be good and decent.

There are different rules for men and women. Men should not wear cloth such as silk or clothes decorated with gold. It may make them proud. So fine clothes are only to be worn by women.

Men are expected to cover their body from the navel to their knees. Women are asked to cover their whole body – except for the face, hands and feet. This can cause problems in a non-Muslim country, as an imam explained:

▶ A Muslim girl can go swimming with other girls. Then the law is relaxed. She can go in a swimming costume with girls and a lady instructor. But swimming with men, there would be a problem.

This Muslim woman is selling Ramadan lights at her shop in Egypt.

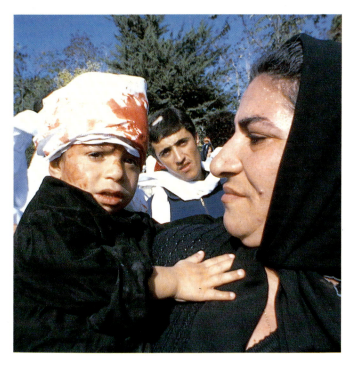

This little boy is a Shi'ite Muslim, living in the Lebanon. During the Ashuva celebrations, which mark the death of the Shi'ite Al-Hussein, some men and boys deliberately injure themselves. Shi'ite Muslims have special respect for those who are prepared to suffer or die for their faith.

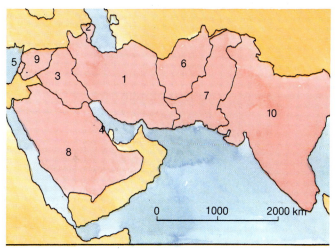

KEY

1. IRAN 93%	6. AFGHANISTAN 35%
2. AZERBAIJAN 59%	7. PAKISTAN 17%
3. IRAQ 57%	8. SAUDI ARABIA 15%
4. BAHREIN 57%	9. SYRIA 4%
5. LEBANON 38%	10. INDIA 2%

Where the Shi'ite Muslims live. The figures show the percentage of the population which is Shi'ite.

All this changed in recent years. Iran is the main home of the Shi'a Muslims. In the 1930s, the ruler of Iran, the Shah, began to make changes in his country. He tried to make it more western. Women were not allowed to cover the face. They had to wear western clothes instead.

Many Shi'a Muslims disliked these changes. In 1979, there was a revolution. The Shah was forced to leave the country. The country was taken over by its religious leaders, called ayatollahs. The word means 'sign of God'.

The leading ayatollah was Ayatollah Khomeini. He made Iran an Islamic state once more. Islamic laws, based on the Qur'an, were introduced. Alcohol was banned. Women could only appear in public with their heads and bodies fully covered.

A true Islamic state is run in the same way that the Prophet Muhammad organised the Muslim community in Madinah. In an Islamic state, the head of state (or a deputy) is supposed to lead the daily prayers at a central mosque. This was how Muhammad led his state. Many Muslims would like to see the practice brought back.

1 Answer these questions in complete sentences:
a) What are the two main Muslim groups called?
b) Which group is the larger?
c) About what did Shi'a and Sunni Muslims disagree?
d) Name one Sunni country and one Shi'ite country.
e) Who are the 'twelvers' and 'seveners'?
f) In which country was there an Islamic revolution in 1979?
g) What were the results of this?
2 a) In groups, work out what you would expect life to be like in an Islamic state. You may need to read earlier chapters again to remind yourself of some ideas.
b) How would it be different from life in Britain today?
c) Now, compare your answers to (a) and (b). What do you think a Muslim would miss most by living in Britain?

20 Islam's Gifts to the World

Some scientific instruments developed by Muslims.

The Qur'an encourages Muslims to seek for knowledge. So early Muslim rulers did the same. As a result, Muslims made great contributions to science and mathematics.

Much of their knowledge was needed for religious reasons. They needed to know the hours for prayer. Payment of zakat meant they had to do mathematics.

Arabs brought Arabic numerals (such as 1 and 2) to Europe; Arabs were the first to use zero. More than that, Muslim scholars were the first to work out a full system of decimal calculation. Europeans later took up the idea. Muslims also invented algebra.

Muslim scientists showed special interest in **astronomy** and the stars. They needed to be able to work out the direction of Makkah so that they could pray wherever they were.

As a result, they discovered many 'new' stars. Europeans still call some today by their Arabic names. They also invented the astrolabe which measures the height of the stars. Western explorers found this useful on their voyages of discovery.

Muslim scientists learned by experiments. In the middle ages, the Christian Church discouraged western scientists from carrying out experiments. So Muslim scientists took the lead in geography and botany.

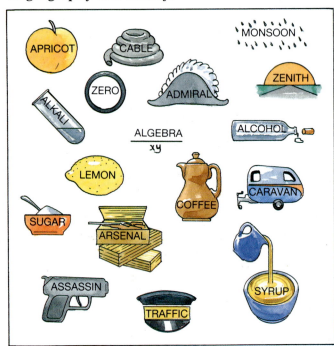

Just some of the Arabic words we still use today.

In medicine, Muslim doctors were more skilled than Christian ones. They relied less on surgery and more on natural drugs and herbs. They stressed good diet and a healthy life. Today, many non-Muslims still turn to Muslim healers for natural treatment of illnesses.

Muslim traders travelled far overseas long before western explorers such as Columbus. Their maps were some of the finest of their time. Their earliest world maps show the earth as round. Most Europeans of the time still thought it was flat.

Many books written by ancient Greeks and Romans survive only because they were copied and translated by Muslims. Muslim **scholars** travelled throughout Europe, tracking down ancient **manuscripts**. In turn, people from all over Europe travelled to Muslim universities. Muslims were ahead of Europeans in almost every branch of knowledge.

Muslims have had a tradition of making carpets for well over a thousand years. Muslim tents had little furniture. They had cushions and rugs instead.

Many Muslims today have their own beautiful prayer mats. Often, carpet-weavers base the whole decoration around a single word, woven over and over again. It is always possible to spot one which has been woven by a Muslim. This carpet expert explains:

▶ In any true Persian or Turkish rug, it should be possible to discover the Deliberate Mistake. Many of the Muslim faith believe that only Allah makes things perfectly; therefore, to weave a perfectly designed rug would be to risk offending Him.

I once knew a repairer of rugs who held this belief so firmly that he was in constant trouble with his employer. Just before finishing work on each rug, he would make a deliberate mistake. He explained that, although he was afraid of offending his employer, he was even more fearful of offending Allah.

Caroline Bosly: *Rugs to Riches*

A Muslim prayer mat. The compass is used to work out the direction of Makkah. The booklet gives prayer times around the world.

1 Copy out and fill in the grid below, using the clues.
a) Muslims practically invented this.
b) This Arabic word is still used to mean nought.
c) Muslim doctors stressed this.
d) Muslim scholars worked out a system of _____ calculation.
e) The study of the stars.
f) Muslim scientists took the lead in this.

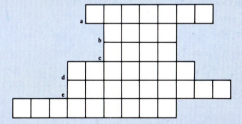

2 You need a sheet of squared paper. Design a mat, based on either Arabic writing or the design you can see on the mat opposite. It should be suitable for using as a prayer mat.

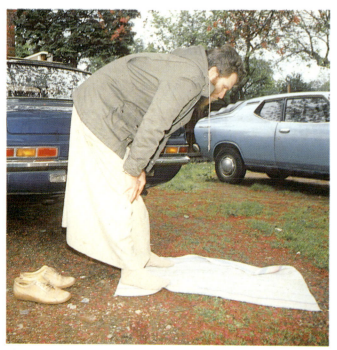

Many western people have become Muslims in recent years. This man, praying in the open air, is one of them.

No one knows exactly how many Muslims there are in the world today. But we do know that Islam is the second largest religion after Christianity and it is the world's fastest-growing religion.

Yet, for most of the last 200 years, it was very different. In the 18th and 19th centuries most Muslim countries were under western control. By contrast with Europe, Muslim countries were poor.

Since the second world war, most Muslim countries have become independent once more. Many have become richer by selling oil. So Muslims have once again become a powerful force in world affairs. Islam is once again spreading. Muslims believe this is a gift from God.

Other world powers discovered the power of Islam in 1973 when Israel was at war with Egypt and Syria, both of which are Arab countries. The Arabs were supported by most other Muslim countries. They objected to Israel having land which had once been Arab. They also objected to the United States supporting Israel.

So they used a new weapon to support Egypt and Syria. They stopped selling oil to the United States. The result was a world oil shortage. Almost overnight, prices trebled.

When the ban ended, the Arabs made it clear that they would use oil as a political weapon again, if they chose. After two centuries of being controlled by the west, the Muslims felt that at last they would be taken seriously.

The revival of Islam is seen most clearly in Iran, which did not join in the 1973 **boycott**. After the 1979 revolution, a large number of the people voted to set up an Islamic state. This means that their laws are based on the Qur'an.

Many Iranians were pleased with the changes. Politics is part of their religion. They believe that, if the state follows religious laws, its political problems will be solved. But not all Muslim countries approved. In 1980, Iraq and Iran began a war which went on until 1988.

What made the Iranian revolution special was that its leaders wanted Shi'ite groups elsewhere to fight for power, too. So Iran supported Shi'ite groups in other countries, such as the Lebanon.

Iranian soldiers at prayer during the war with Iraq. Some Muslims claim that the Iranian revolution was political, not religious.

Muslims from many different countries gather at the Regent's Park mosque in London.

Iran would like to see all Muslims living under strict Islamic rule.

The Iranian revolution worried many non-Muslim countries. In the Soviet Union, the Muslim population is growing fast. One in five of the world's Muslims lives there. Its leaders have been worried that Soviet Muslims might demand the right to rule themselves by Islamic law.

The revolution put Islam back into the spotlight. Muslims believe that when all Muslims around the world come together, the world will be a more peaceful place.

If that happens, perhaps one of the old Muslim sayings will come true. It compares Muslims around the world to a single body. When one part of it aches, the whole body feels the effect and rushes to help.

1 a) If everybody were the same religion, would the world be at peace? Explain your answer.
b) Why do you think people of the same religion still have disagreements?
2 a) Why do you think some westerners are choosing to become Muslims?
b) From what you have read, suggest three major changes this would mean in their lives.

3 Iran and Iraq are both Muslim countries, yet they went to war. Does this mean:
a) their leaders are not good Muslims or
b) Islam does not believe in peace? Explain both your answers.
4 Design a suitable flag for Iran after it became an Islamic state. When you have finished, you could compare your efforts with the real thing.

Connections

1 Word search

This square includes words which were used in the first twelve chapters of this book. They may read forwards or backwards, and across, down or sideways. Each time you find a word write it down and explain what it means.

2 Where am I?

Six Muslims are pictured below. Each is talking about a place he or she is visiting. Each place is important to Muslims. For each one, write down where you think the person is.

```
A L L A H O Q U R A N M
D H A C A L I P H R Y U
H A R D B M J E Q I L H
A B A M A O J J A H E A
N T F M K S A I S L A M
H U A L A Q H A K K A M
A H T W E U M E D I N A
M K M T T E M U E U Z D
A R N A D A M A R D A L
Q U K L E I R B A G E H
I A H A J I D A H K L P
Z A S S E R D A M K H A
```

1. If I can get close enough, I shall kiss the stone.

2. Have you got your pebbles ready to throw?

3. So this is where the Angel Gabriel appeared to Muhammad.

4. I'm glad we came. I always wanted to see where Muhammad ran the first Islamic community.

5. Muhammad gave his last sermon here.

6. I'm exhausted already. Just think how tired Hagar must have been.

Glossary

Allah – the Muslim name for God
assembly – meeting
astronomy – study of the sun, moon, stars, etc
atom – tiny bit

Bedouin – Arab who lives in the desert and has no fixed home
bereaved – deprived (of relations)
boycott – refuse to buy or sell

chaplain – priest in duty at an institution, such as a hospital or prison
civil war – war between people of the same country
clot – mass which is partly solid
compassionate – pitying
compulsion – use of force
compulsory – compelled; required
congregation – meeting of people for worship

descendant – person born into a family, eg child or grandchild
devotion – deep love

empire – group of countries ruled by another country
extended family – family which has more than just parents and their children living together

foster-mother – woman who brings up another woman's child

humility – not being proud

identical – exactly the same
idol – thing that is worshipped, such as a statue
imam – person who leads the prayers in a mosque
incite – urge; encourage
interest – extra cost of borrowing money

Ka'bah – cube-like building in Makkah towards which Muslims pray

legend – ancient story which many people believed

manuscript – book written by hand
meditating – thinking deeply
mosaic – small pieces of stone which make a pattern
mosque – Muslim building for prayer and worship

niche – hollow in a wall

orphan – child whose parents are dead
orthodox – views accepted by most people

pagan – person who worshipped many gods
participate – take part
pilgrim – person on a religious journey to a holy place
prejudiced – having opinions without good reasons
prophet – person who speaks out in the name of God
prostration – bowing down low

recite – say aloud from memory

sacred – holy
sacrificed – offered to God
Satan – the Devil
scholar – person who has a great deal of knowledge
sermon – public talk on religion
shrine – sacred place
sin – doing something wrong
submission – obedience to a greater power
Sura Yasin – a chapter of the Qur'an
symbolic – used as a symbol (sign) of something else

temperament – what a person is like

vision – something seen

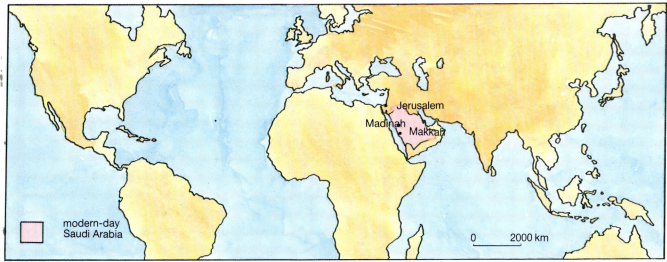

The area where Muhammad lived.

call it the hijra, which means departure. Even today, the Muslim system of dating years starts with Muhammad's journey. So the Islamic calendar starts in 622CE (1AH).

In Madinah, Muhammad started the first Muslim community. The first **mosque** was built there and Muhammad's house was next door. Muhammad himself even helped to build the mosque. He taught that everyone was equal in the eyes of God. He mended his own clothes and did his own shopping. He wanted to be a good example to his people.

► A woman came with a garment which she had made especially for the Prophet. He gracefully accepted it and wore it. Coming to an **assembly** he was met by a man who touched it and said, 'Give it to me, O Messenger of God'. The Prophet said, 'With pleasure!' Having stayed for some time at the meeting, he went home, took off the garment, wrapped it up and sent it to the man who asked for it, [although] he was in sore need of it himself.

Yathrib was later called Madinah-al-Nabi – the City of the Prophet. Today, it is still called Madinah (Medina). This green dome is built there above Muhammad's tomb.

1 Write one sentence about each of these words: prophet; vision; idol; pagan; shrine; Satan; hijra.

2 a) In the cave picture, which person is Satan?
   b) What weapon is he carrying?
   c) What have *two* creatures made in front of the cave?
   d) Why would this make the soldiers think that Muhammad was not inside?

3 a) Work in pairs. One of you is from Yathrib and the other is one of Muhammad's followers. The person from Yathrib is trying to persuade the Muslim to come to Yathrib. Write down their conversation. (You could tape record the conversation between the two of them.)

4 a) Still in pairs, write an obituary notice for Muhammad. One of you writes what a Muslim might have written. The other writes what a merchant from Makkah might have written.
   b) Now, compare your obituaries. What differences are there – and why?

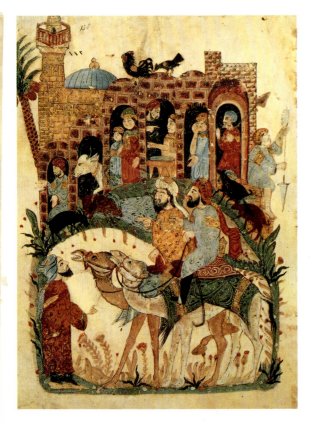

These Muslim travellers are being welcomed as they pass through a Syrian town in the 13th century.

The Arabic letters SLM mean peace and obedience.

The great Arab Muslim empire was destroyed in the 13th century. But Islam itself went on spreading. In Africa, Muslim traders carried Muhammad's message south far beyond the Muslim empire.

Trade also took Islam across the Indian Ocean. Muslim merchants had for years been spreading their beliefs east in Malaysia and Indonesia. A chain of towns was set up down the east coast of Africa 500 years before Portuguese explorers arrived – and destroyed them.

The Arab commander Khalid besieged Damascus. When the people gave in, he told them this:

▶ In the name of Allah, the **compassionate**, the merciful, this is what Khalid ibn al-Walid would grant to the people of Damascus . . . He promises to give them security for their lives, property and churches. Their city wall shall not be demolished. No Muslim shall be quartered in their houses. We give to them the pact of Allah and the protection of His Prophet . . . So long as they pay the tax, nothing but good shall befall them.

1 Match up the words on the left with the correct meanings from the right.

Ka'bah	Muslims' holy book
Qur'an	the religion of Muslims
Abu Bakr	cube-shaped building in Makkah
Islam	Muhammad's successor

2 a) Look at the map on page 8. Using an atlas, write down the names of at least eight modern countries which were part of the Muslim empire.
b) Write down any of these eight countries which are not mainly Muslim today.

3 a) Why did Muhammad want people to become Muslims?
b) Why do you think Muslims wanted to spread their religion?
c) Why didn't they force Christians or Jews to become Muslims?
d) Read what Khalid said to the people of Damascus. Do you think he was being fair? Give reasons.

4 Design a pattern around the letters SLM and the words ISLAM and MUSLIM. Your design should give an idea of peace.

9

4 Holy Book – the Qur'an

> ► And He (commands you, saying): This is my straight path, so follow it. Do not follow other paths, which will separate you from His path. This He has ordered you so that you may be truly obedient.
>
> Qur'an 6:153

The holy book for Muslims is called the Qur'an. Muslims believe it is the word of God, exactly as the Angel Gabriel revealed it to Muhammad. It was not revealed all at once to Muhammad, but in parts over 23 years.

As Muhammad could not write, he chose people to write it down. Few other Arabs could read in those days either but they did have a gift for learning long stories and poems by heart.

Today, all Muslims learn parts of the Qur'an by heart. Some people can **recite** it all. Such a person is called a hafiz. The Qur'an contains about 78 000 words. (This book has less than 20 000).

After Muhammad's death, many Muslims were killed in battle. Abu Bakr was worried that the Qur'an might be lost. So he ordered a standard copy to be made. This was checked by those who had heard it direct from Muhammad himself. This copy was made less than two years after Muhammad died. All modern copies are the same as this.

The book was revealed to Muhammad in Arabic, a language which most Muslims can still read. Muslims do not believe it is possible to translate it perfectly. In any case, it is a beautiful book and the beauty becomes lost in any other language.

A true Muslim reads the Qur'an every day. It gives guidance for everyone on how to live a good life. It explains how to serve God. Muslims believe it is the final word of God to human beings, and that it is therefore perfect.

Because they believe that the Qur'an contains the actual words of God, Muslims treat it with great respect. Before reading it, they first wash themselves. Copies of the Qur'an are kept wrapped up and often put on a shelf to keep them safe.

Although the Qur'an is the Muslims' holy book, they also consult books called the Hadith. These are collections of the words and actions of

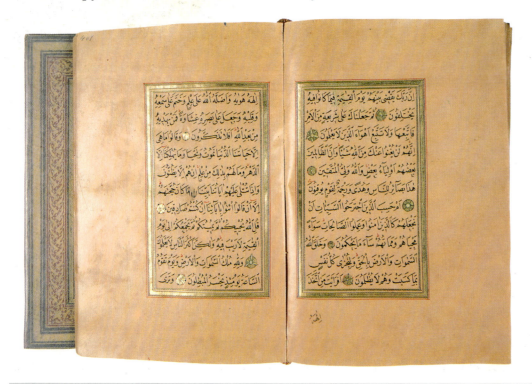

There are two original copies of the Qur'an in the world today. This one is kept in Istanbul. The Qur'an is divided into 114 chapters, called suras. The first ones are the longest.

The Qur'an contains 99 names of God. These are some of them.

Muhammad himself. If Muslims face a problem, they may well read the Hadith to see if Muhammad ever coped with a similar problem. Then, they could follow his advice.

Muslims believe that the Qur'an is God's message. That message tells them that there is only one God who created the world and everything in it. In the Qur'an, he provides his followers with a complete set of rules for daily life. This is how one Muslim teenager describes it.

► It tells us what the right things are and what the wrong things are. It tells us what to do and what not to do. So that way we keep the straight path. We've got the Qur'an to guide us and we've got the prophet Muhammad's sayings. So it helps us.

We asked some Muslims for their favourite part of the Qur'an. This is what a young woman said:

► I read **Sura Yasin** every day. People say it helps to make the day go by very easily. It is called 'the heart of the Qur'an'. The Prophet encouraged Muslims to read this chapter regularly.

This is what an **imam** said:

► Some chapters are favourite to me because they're very telling. For instance, we have a chapter called the Quraish. It refers to the tribe where the Prophet actually was born and he mentioned two major blessings – free from hunger and free from fear. I find this situation really the most important in people's lives.

All Muslims are expected to read the Qur'an and learn at least some of it by heart.

1 Answer these questions in complete sentences:
a) What is the holy book of Islam called?
b) In what language is it written?
c) Why do Muslims believe it is holy?
d) Why do you think Muslims read it every day?

2 a) How do Muslims show their respect for the Qur'an? (Your should find at least three answers.)
b) How else could they show their respect?

3 a) Read the quotation from the Qur'an. What do you think the 'straight path' is?

b) How did the Imam pick his favourite passage from the Qur'an?
c) Does this mean that he and the young woman read the Qur'an for different reasons? Explain your answer.

4 a) Look at the different names of God. How can God be all these different things?
b) Three other names of God are the wise, the protector and the peace. Write out these words, as our artist has, to give an idea of their meaning.

5 *What Muslims Believe*

Muslims are expected to believe – *and act on their beliefs*. It is not enough just to believe or just to act. A Muslim's actions are based on the following beliefs.

One god (Allah)

Islam teaches that there is only one God. He has no family or partners. He is the only one whom people should worship. Every day, a Muslim says several times: 'There is no god but Allah and Muhammad is His Messenger.'

▶ O my dear son! Do not make any partner to Allah. Truly, making anyone partner to Allah is a big **sin**.

Qur'an 31:13

His angels

Angels are God's servants who carry out His orders. They brought God's message to the prophets, including Muhammad himself. Other angels spend their time keeping records of human actions. But they cannot be seen by us.

These Muslims are praying in a street in Seneghal.

His books

Muslims believe that God has given all humans guidance through his prophets. There have been a number of holy books, including the Old and New Testaments. But only the Qur'an has not been changed by human beings. So only the Qur'an is perfect and will never change. The Qur'an is therefore the final word of God.

His prophets

The Qur'an mentions 25 prophets by name. Most of them also appear in the Bible. The first was Adam and the last was Muhammad. Muslims believe they were all sent by God to show people how He wanted them to live.

The Day of Judgment

When this day comes, all dead people will come to life and be questioned about their lives. It will not be the effect of their actions that matters; it will be what people *intended* their actions should do.

Index

Abraham   24, 25, 34
Abu Bakr   8, 10
Adam   12, 24
Adhan   26
Ali   40
Angel Gabriel   6, 10
angels   12
aqiqah   26
Arafat, Mount   35
Arafat, Valley of   24
Ashura   35
Azerbaijan   40

Bangladesh   26
Bedouins   4, 33
birth   26–7

Caliph   8, 40

Damascus   9
Day of Judgment   12–13, 27
death   27
dowry   29
Du'ah   14

Egypt   15, 38, 44
Eid-ul-Adha   34–5
Eid-ul-Fitr   34

Hadith   11, 13, 20
hafiz   10
Hagar   24
halal   38
hajj   24–25, 27
Hell   13
hijra   6
Hira, Mount   5

imam   15, 18, 19, 30, 37, 40
Indonesia   9, 35
Iqamah   26
Iran   36, 40, 41, 44, 45
Iraq   31, 44
Ishmael   24, 25, 34

Ka'bah   4, 6, 8, 16, 24, 25, 27
Kenya   36
Khadijah   4
Khalid   9
Khomeini, Ayatollah   41

Lailat ul Qadr   23, 35
Lebanon   40, 41, 44

Madinah   6, 7, 8, 14, 25, 41
madressa   19
Makkah   4, 5, 6, 8, 14, 16, 24, 27, 42, 47
Malaysia   9, 13, 29
marriage   28–9
mihrab   17
minaret   16
minbar   17
Morocco   28
Moses   35
mosques   7, 13, 14, 15, 16–17, 18, 23, 26
muezzin   16
Muzdalifah   24

Nigeria   19
Noah   35

Oman   33

Paradise   13, 32

Quraish   11
Qur'an   8, 10–11, 12, 17, 18, 19, 23, 27, 28, 29, 30, 31, 32, 34, 35, 36, 41, 42, 44

Ramadan   5, 22, 23, 34, 38

Salat   14, 39
Saudi Arabia   4, 32, 39, 40
sawm   22–23
Seneghal   11
Shi'ite muslims   40, 41, 44
Sunni muslims   40, 45
Syria   4, 44

Tunisia   29

Virgin Mary   32

Yathrib   6, 7

zakat   20–21, 42